THE AUTHOR OF THE UNIVERSE HAS CALLED YOU:

BE TRANSFORMED

THE AUTHOR OF THE UNIVERSE HAS CALLED YOU:

BE TRANSFORMED

CHERYL ST. LOUIS FELIX

CONTENTS

FOREWORD

"All my life" – that's the best phrase I can use to explain how long I've known the author. Cheryl-Ann is the eldest of seven (7) children and growing up together as sisters life did give us our fair share of what we will now appreciate as trials and testimonies. Throughout our growing years none of us would have ever imagined that life's situations and the lessons we learnt would have helped shaped Cheryl-Ann's outlook on life and enrich her with the wisdom she now possesses to be able to use these lessons to help others 'Be Transformed'.

It is very easy to see life's situations as just things that should happen, but it takes someone with a deep passion for wanting to help others appreciate how valuable the lessons we encounter throughout life's journey are meant to help shape us and make us better. We simply need to learn to appreciate even the tiniest lesson from our situations.

Cheryl's wisdom is further enriched by her personal

stories, making this book a relatable and inspiring guide for anyone seeking to navigate life's challenges with grace and fortitude. Her emphasis on the significance of generational legacy, the importance of choosing battles wisely, and the power of embracing lifelong learning are particularly resonant.

This book is a call to embrace the unknown, to trust the process, and to allow oneself to be transformed by the experiences life presents. Through engaging exercises and thought-provoking reflections, readers are encouraged to delve deep into their own journeys, uncovering the values and principles that shape their paths.

As you embark on this transformational journey, I invite you to open your heart and mind to the possibilities that lie ahead. Let this book be a companion and a guide, helping you to unlock your full potential and discover the profound impact of trusting in the next chapter of your life.

Welcome to a journey of reflection, growth, and transformation.

Phenomenal Patty

WINTER

With the golden hues of fall fading into the crisp onset of winter, our journey circles back to its reflective roots. Winter calls us to once again turn inward. This season of closure and fulfillment also reignites the spark of planning and preparation. It's when we lay the groundwork for future endeavors, setting the stage for the transformations that spring will bring. As the world slows down, we're given the perfect backdrop for deep reflection and strategic decision-making.

This is the time to gather by the fire, both literally and metaphorically, to review your past year's journeys and chart new paths. It's a period to prioritize, to sift through your aspirations and determine which battles are worth fighting and where your focus should be sharpened. Winter is your moment to fortify your intentions, ensuring that when the ice melts, and the first green shoots appear, you are ready to spring forward with clarity and purpose.

PREPARATION FOR SUCCESS

PREPARE FOR THE DRIVE

FOCUS ON THE PERMIT - THE VEHICLE WILL COME

My first experience behind the steering wheel was at the age of 10 when my father had an RX. I would ask him, "Daddy, show me how to drive?" and he would allow me to drive it into the garage and reverse out. It felt good. I knew that one day I needed to have a car, so I equated having a driver's permit with having a car. I remember by the time I was 20 years old my uncle said to me, "Why don't you get your license?" I would respond, "I don't have a job so the chances are I am not going to get a vehicle anytime soon".

My uncle looked at me and said, "Don't focus on the vehicle; get the license and the vehicle will come." I eventually got my driver's license and, of course, years later I bought my first vehicle, but prior to ownership I became the trusted driver for friends, entrusted with their vehicles for errands and post-party drives. The open road welcomed me because I was prepared.

Many of us harbor dreams—to be a star footballer, a chief accountant, a CEO, an entrepreneur, a musician, or a freelancer. But do we lay the groundwork for success? It's not about luck; it's about readiness when the moment arrives. Whether it's the scout on the field or the job vacancy requiring specific qualifications, preparation is the key to seizing opportunities.

REFLECTIVE CHALLENGE

Reflect on the areas in your life where you may be waiting for the perfect opportunity to arise. List the steps you need to take to achieve them. Consider what you can do now to start laying the groundwork for your future success. Challenge yourself to find joy and fulfillment in the process itself, even before reaching the final outcome.

INTERACTIVE EXERCISE

Identify your long-term goals and the short-term actions needed to achieve them. Share your goals with a partner, friend or mentor for accountability.

TRANSFORMATION/ RESULTS

In the pursuit of dreams, the lesson remains clear: focus on obtaining your permit—the skills, qualifications, and readiness required for your ambitions. Trust that when the road stretches out before you, you'll be prepared to drive into the opportunities that await. As you lay the groundwork for success, you will find fulfillment not only in reaching your goals but also in the journey itself, enjoying each step along the way.

THE TOOLBOX

A young man, for one month, visited a carpenter's shop. He was impressed with the lovely handiwork completed by the man. The carpenter was working on an item, and every day he would inquire what it was, and the carpenter's response would always be the same: "All I can say is it is beautiful and will be a treasure to someone." In the first three days the young man looked on, he would just observe all that the carpenter was doing. On the fourth day, he started to assist the carpenter by moving pieces of wood and handing the carpenter his tools. The first day the carpenter requested a Phillips screwdriver, the young man brought a hammer. The next time he asked for a sander, the young man brought a measuring tape. The carpenter realized the young man had no idea of the tools and what they were used for. Every time he sent him for a tool, he would tell him what it was useful for. One day, the carpenter was working on a piece of wood. He asked for the measuring tape, measured the piece of wood, marked a spot, and asked for the chisel. He started to chisel away the wood. He chiseled for about one hour, then asked for the sander. That also took him some time. The young man wondered how long it would take before the carpenter would finish this piece of wood. Sometimes the carpenter would step away from the piece of wood, sit, look like he was pondering, and then ask for a particular tool, return to the piece of wood, and continue to work on it. After three days, the carpenter looked satisfied and placed the wood with the other pieces he had completed. A month passed, and the pieces of wood were now being put together. The young man couldn't believe his eyes. He never would have imagined such a beautiful item.

For years, the young man stayed with the carpenter. The carpenter gave him his first measuring tape. Thereafter, the young man received a hammer and other items he could use. Three years later, the young man started to take private jobs. He would visit the carpenter to share his accomplishments and sometimes seek advice on his carpentry. The carpenter always asked two questions: first, what he was trying to accomplish, i.e., what is the look and feel you want,and secondly, what tool would you have to use to get you that look and feel. Every time the carpenter had finished, the young man would leave with his head down, feeling dejected, but return later smiling and advising that he worked it out.

For several years, he visited the carpenter, and although he was trained by the carpenter, his clientele was different from the carpenter's. He always ensured that the customer was always satisfied. One day, a client requested a particular item; he knew he could make it. So, quietly, he studied all that he needed and started to put the things together. However, he reached a critical part of the item and couldn't figure out what had to be done. He could no longer go to the carpenter because he had passed away, and within days after his death, his tool shop burnt to the ground. Days he would watch the piece of wood and couldn't move on it. Then, one day the words of the carpenter came to him, "what look and feel are you trying to get, and what tool will get you that?". He thought about all the tools in his toolbox and brought them out. He started to consider which was appropriate, and over the next two days he finished the item. The client was very pleased.

REFLECTIVE CHALLENGE

Take a moment to reflect on your own journey of apprenticeship. Consider the mentors and teachers who have guided you along the way, providing you with the tools and wisdom needed to navigate life's challenges. What lessons have you learned from them, and how have they shaped your journey thus far?

INTERACTIVE EXERCISE

Identify one area of your life where you feel like an apprentice, eager to learn and grow. Write down three tools or resources you can utilize to further your understanding and skill in this area. Then, commit to incorporating these tools into your daily practice, seeking guidance and mentorship as needed. Share your progress with a trusted friend or mentor, and together celebrate the journey of learning and growth.

TRANSFORMATION/ RESULTS

In life, we each have a toolbox with tools from those around us. The question is: What are you trying to achieve in life? What is the look and feel you want and which tools will help you achieve that? The tools of values, patience, love, prayers, faith, commitment, listening. Whatever the tools in your toolbox -use them.

A JOURNEY IN LEADERSHIP

Did you know that control involves self-discipline, perseverance, and a proactive approach to life's challenges?

In the whirlwind of burnout and uncertainty, I found myself navigating the unpredictable currents of life's journey. As a leader, the urge to delegate or abandon ship loomed large, but the inclusive leadership path held its own uncertainties and tests.

Amid travel delays and disrupted plans, I embraced the opportunity to learn from the universe or, as I preferred to believe, the Creator. Leadership, I realized, wasn't about devouring the entire elephant but focusing on manageable bites, passing the torch to the next person at the table.

Amid headaches and muscle spasms, mental realignment became crucial. Seeking direction and following through, I received a clear message: I wouldn't arrive for the meeting's opening, but I would reach at lunch, enjoy the journey, and fulfill my leadership responsibilities.

True to the guidance, flight delays and missed connections became part of the adventure. Engaging with retired individuals during the trip, sharing moments and stories, offered unexpected connections. An encounter with a spirited senior on the plane, guiding me to stretch and bringing unexpected joy, highlighted the beauty of spontaneous connections.

In the airport hustle, I navigated a new process, adapting swiftly to the unfamiliar airport. Reassigned to a middle seat at the gate, disappointment crept in. Yet, between snoring and coughing seatmates, I found moments to write my thoughts into this story.

By the time I checked into my hotel, the headaches had dissipated, and relaxation settled in. As I reflected on the day's events, I realized that life's uncomfortable rides aren't always about us; they're opportunities to sprinkle our goodness on others.

Life's journey, I was reminded, often picks us up for uncomfortable rides, but it's not solely about us. It's about the people we meet along the way, the chance to share a smile, and the encouragement to trust the next chapter of our lives.

REFLECTIVE CHALLENGE

Explore your mindset towards uncertainty and unexpected challenges. Reflect on how you typically respond to disrupted plans and unexpected events. Consider how you can cultivate a proactive approach to embracing uncertainty and learning from life's twists and turns.

INTERACTIVE EXERCISE

Challenge yourself to initiate spontaneous connections with others during your daily interactions. Strike up conversations with strangers, share moments of joy, and embrace unexpected encounters as opportunities for meaningful connections.

TRANSFORMATION/RESULTS

Cultivate resilience by embracing uncertainty and learning from life's challenges. Develop a proactive mindset that enables you to navigate unpredictable situations with confidence and grace. Experience deepened connections with others as you embrace spontaneous interactions and

share moments of joy and encouragement along life's journey. Build a sense of community and support that enriches
your personal and professional life.

UNBURDENING THE SHORE OF THE SOUL

FORGIVENESS PART I

One Sunday, I visited the beach to collect some Sargassum weeds and observed the turbulent Atlantic Ocean, which provoked my reflections on possession, forgiveness, and the metaphorical shores of the soul. The sight of unkempt beachfronts, strewn with Sargassum weeds, unveils parallels with the profound act of forgiving.

As the Sargassum weeds washed ashore, the beachfront appeared disheveled, even uninviting. Research unveiled the paradox that Sargassum, when losing its buoyancy, provides energy to deep-sea organisms while also cleansing shorelines. I collected the Sargassum because it provided beneficial nutrients to my plants, though it seemed unattractive on the shoreline. The act of collecting the weeds reminded me of the role of forgiveness. Despite the initial unattractiveness, the sargassum weeds contribute to the growth and well-being of another entity. Similarly, forgiveness, though challenging, holds transformative potential.

REFLECTIVE CHALLENGE

Pause and reflect on an area in your life where forgiveness may appear challenging or unattractive. Examine the range of emotions you felt during the situation: anger, resentment, shame, anxiety, disappointment, etc.

TRANSFORMATION/RESULTS

The ability to forgive and the reciprocal experience of being forgiven. Embracing forgiveness unburdens the shores of the soul, paving the way for stability, peace, and transformative growth.

CHOOSING WISELY

FORGIVENESS PART II
A JOURNEY TO LIBERATION

We continue this week's series on forgiveness. Let us discuss why forgive? I always thought that forgiveness was easy for me until it had come so close that it seemed impossible, or probably I was unwilling. I felt betrayed and robbed. Betrayed because I never thought the individual could betray me or betray what they themselves said they believed, and robbed because I felt like my opportunity for an experience was stolen. I enjoy looking youthful and refuse to age prematurely.

For me, forgiveness releases a burden that seems to weigh heavily and decreases the spate of my gray hairs. I have come to understand that people will always be people, and sometimes they disappoint not just you but even themselves.

Forgiveness sometimes can be difficult, but through this particular experience I:

- Examined how it pained—I took time to feel it in every way I could: anger, anxiety, shame, disappointment.
- Examined what was the root cause of my pain, this took a while for me to identify the exact reason.
- Examined whether I contributed to this pain directly or indirectly, and

I concluded that everyone has choices, and the choices we make reflect our character at the time of our decisions.

Thereafter, I had a conversation because, in my case, I always prefer to chat rather than to speculate. I must always be able to say that you said this or that because I questioned whether the apologies were genuine.

Then I made a choice. I decided to get up, shake up, and move on. I can't hold onto unforgiveness too long, as I do not wish to put my hair through premature greying, and unforgiveness impacts our physical health immensely.

REFLECTIVE EXERCISE

Write down the specific situation or event that triggered your feelings of pain or resentment.

Statement:

Why 1. Ask yourself why this situation is causing you distress, write down your initial response.

Answer:

Why 2. Ask yourself why your response above is causing you distress. Write down your response.

Answer:

Why 3. Ask yourself why your response above is causing you distress. Write down your response.

Answer:

Why 4 . Ask yourself why your response above is causing you distress. Write down your response.

Answer:

Why 5. Ask yourself why your response above is causing you distress. Write down your response.

Answer:

Review your responses from Questions 1-5 and identify recurring themes or patterns. Look for commonalities or underlying factors that emerge as the root cause of your pain or resentment.

TRANSFORMATION/ RESULTS

It is important to have clarity and perspective on the underlying causes of your pain. This will assist in emotional liberation and relief.

Through this process of reflective challenges and inter-active exercises, readers experience a release of emotional burden as they confront and process their feelings of resentment and betrayal.

FORGIVENESS PART III

UNLEASHED: THE JOURNEY TO LIBERATION

There is a saying, 'fool me once shame on you, fool me twice shame on me,' Question is who do you forgive, who is worthy of such honour?

I can share that during my experience of betrayal and uncertainty, I had to release and allow things to take their course, knowing that the anchor I hold on to is God, who is stronger and more stable than the anchor of a human being because His promises never wane.

During that period of time, as they say, "time heals all wounds," I realized that after I had identified the pain issues, just letting go and holding on to my surest anchor made it much easier to forgive. To forgive and not even be emotionally negative towards the individual that betrayed me.

Once I had forgiven the person who wronged me, the level of peace I felt within made it easier and more certain that I didn't have to worry about the future. It's so important to forgive. The genuine smile returned, and the genuine laughter returned. The level of peace that followed from genuinely forgiving occurred. I left that chapter with the understanding that humans will always fall, and if you are anchored to a human, the chances are you will go down as well. Lesson learnt, keep your Anchor on God where you are sure to be stable and safe in everything and remain buoyant.

REFLECTIVE EXERCISE

Identify and journal about the anchors you rely on during times of betrayal or uncertainty.

INTERACTIVE EXERCISE

1. Find a quiet and peaceful location near the beach where you can sit comfortably.
2. Set up seating arrangements conducive to meditation, such as cushions or chairs.
3. Close your eyes and take seven (7) deep breaths, allowing your body to relax and your mind to be still.
4. Relax and focus on forgiveness, compassion, and the transformational power of releasing resentment.
5. Listen to the sound of waves crashing gently against the shore.
6. Feel the warmth of the sun on your skin and the soft sand beneath your feet.
7. Bring to mind the individual who has caused you the pain or resentment.

8. Think of them in your mind with compassion, acknowledging their humanity and the complexity of their own struggles and suffering.
9. Now you will say a series of affirmations or phrases focused on forgiveness, such as, I release any resentment or anger I hold towards [person's name]. I wish them peace and healing.
10. Visualize forgiveness as a healing light that surrounds both you and the person you are forgiving, bringing a sense of peace and closure to the situation.
11. For seven minutes of silence, cultivate feelings of forgiveness and compassion towards yourself and the person or persons.
12. Now, breathe slowly seven times, open your eyes, and smile.
13. Journal any insights or emotions that arose during the meditation.
14. Then, say a brief statement of gratitude or an affirmation of compassion and forgiveness.

TRANSFORMATION/ RESULTS

By letting go of resentment and embracing forgiveness, you will experience a shift in mindset that allows you to move forward with greater clarity, purpose, and compassion.

A GOOD FRIEND OR A GOOD SERVANT

A good servant works for you. A good servant does everything for his master and for a reward, whether it be money, promotion, or even acknowledgment—that's a good servant.

A good friend works with you. A good friend keeps you and helps you. A good friend is one you can expose all your vulnerabilities to, and they wouldn't take advantage of it. You can't do that with a good servant because the chances are they will use that against you sometime in the future, especially if they feel unfairness.

Friendship can be so fickle, especially if it's not a good friendship. A good friend sees what opportunities are for you and helps you maneuver through them. A good friend helps you with your growth; a good friend covers your faults.

REFLECTIVE EXERCISE

Take time to reflect on past friendships or current relationships in your life. Consider the qualities and behaviors that made those relationships positive or negative experiences. Ask yourself what qualities you value most in a friend and how they align with your past experiences. Next, assess your current circle of friends and acquaintances. Reflect on the dynamics of these relationships and whether they exhibit the qualities of a good friend as described in the story. Consider how each relationship contributes to your growth, support, and overall well-being. Finally, reflect on your own needs, vulnerabilities, and boundaries in relationships. Consider what you expect from a good friend and what behaviors are unacceptable. Clarify your boundaries and priorities to better recognize when someone embodies the qualities of a good friend.

INTERACTIVE EXERCISE

Create a list of the top seven qualities that you believe make a good friend, such as trustworthiness, loyalty, empathy, and supportiveness. Rate each quality based on its importance to you on a scale of 1 to 10.

Reflect on why each quality is important and how it contributes to a fulfilling friendship.

Use this inventory to evaluate your current friendships and identify areas for improvement.

TRANSFORMATION/ RESULTS

By fostering friendships built on trust, support, and mutual respect, you will experience greater emotional fulfillment and support in your lives. When you cultivate meaningful friendships based on authenticity and reciprocity, you are more likely to experience personal growth and development.

SENTIMENTAL INVESTMENTS

DISCARD OR REPAIR

I received a watch as a gift and it wasn't a very expensive watch but it was of sentimental value, because of who gave me the watch . Three months into having the watch I had to repair it because for some reason one hand stopped moving. This watch that didn't cost more than $20 to purchase , cost me about $12 for its first repair.

Four to six months later, the watch straps broke off and had to be replaced. This would cost me another $20. The thing is, I looked at it and I wondered, do I want to invest in repairing this watch or do I just want to leave it there? The investment in repairing it seemed much more than the value of the watch. Sometimes in life, there are things that we can put value to and it costs us much more. Your children. How much did it cost you to bring them into this world? How much does it cost you to put a value on who they are? Is it easier to discard the relationship than to invest in it? Is it easier to discard that job or to invest in it for your own skills?. Some things are more sentimental than others.

43

REFLECTIVE CHALLENGE

Reflect on the potential long-term benefits and costs of repairing or preserving sentimental possessions or relationships. How does investing in sentimentality contribute to personal growth, emotional well-being, or meaningful connections? Reflect on whether certain investments align with your values and long-term goals.

INTERACTIVE EXERCISE

In your journal, list three possessions or relationships with sentimental value. Reflect on the emotional significance and whether the investment aligns with their perceived value. Share your insights with a friend or family member, discussing the delicate balance between sentimentality and practicality.

TRANSFORMATION/ RESULTS

You will become empowered to make intentional decisions about repairing or disposing of sentimental possessions or relationships. You will learn to balance emotional attachment with practical considerations, enabling you to prioritize investments that align with your values and long-term goals.

CHOOSING YOUR
BATTLES

In the exuberance of youth, I was swift to respond to every uttered word, a habit rooted in an absence of discipline. However, with age came wisdom, and a valuable lesson was imparted by a colleague-turned-friend: "Pick your battles." Life, much like a battlefield, presents countless engagements, but not every skirmish warrants our participation.

We enter this world on a battlefield, born into the complexities of life. Throughout our journey, we encounter battles—some are battles of anxiety, battles against the backdrop of illness, and numerous challenges that beckon us to engage. Yet, the ultimate objective is clear: to emerge victorious in the war that defines our purpose.

Not every battle demands our attention. The intricacies of life involve battles in work, relationships, internal struggles, and even teenage turmoil. It's imperative to discern which battles align with our purpose and contribute meaningfully to our personal development.

REFLECTIVE CHALLENGE

Take a moment to reflect on the battles you are currently fighting in different aspects of your life (work, relationships, internal struggles). Categorize them into meaningful and unnecessary. What consumes your energy and focus? Which of these align with your purpose and are worth your energy and time?

INTERACTIVE EXERCISE

Imagine your ideal life journey. What battles did you fight, and which ones did you choose to avoid? This will help you gain clarity on your priorities. Discuss with a friend what's truly important.

TRANSFORMATION/ RESULTS

In the journey of life, select your battles with intention. Is it worth the fight, the energy, the emotions? Whether it's work, relationships, or internal struggles, be discerning. Not every battle is yours, but the battles you choose should contribute to your purpose. You will achieve great clarity and focus, directing energy toward more meaningful pursuits.

"SHH": THE POWER OF A SECRET

A talk show host stated that a secret is only a secret if you keep it to yourself. I adopted this practice in my life. A secret was only a secret if I kept it to myself. Because even if I shared something that I considered to be a secret to one person, whom I may consider that I can trust, the chances are, they may share it with one other person whom they think they can trust. That secret may be shared verbatim or a story, even though there will be no identifying factors to the process. Some secrets take longer than others to be released, but sooner or later, they are. I recall a few years ago when I broke my practice and decided to share a secret with a friend, someone I thought would have my back at that very moment. But within 24 hours, the secret returned to me through another source, as a query. You see, the thing is, when you share a secret and you share it with one person, you can easily detect a breach, as they were the only conduit , once no one else was in earshot of the secret at the time of course. Whether the people they told were expected to keep the secret was not the question. The question is, why did you not keep the secret? Sometimes it is good to keep your secret to yourself until you accomplish your goal, or your goal comes to fruition. Can you keep a secret?

REFLECTIVE CHALLENGE

Take a moment to reflect on your relationship with secrets. Consider the secrets you've entrusted to others and those you've held close to your chest. How have these secrets shaped your interactions with others and influenced your sense of trust? Reflect on a time when you shared a secret with someone and the outcome of that decision. Did the act of sharing bring you closer together or create distance? What lessons did you learn from that experience?

INTERACTIVE EXERCISE

Think of a secret you've been carrying, whether it's a personal aspiration, a dream, or a piece of information you've been hesitant to share. Reflect on why you've chosen to keep this secret and the potential impact of revealing it to others. Consider the level of trust you have in those around you and whether they are deserving of your confidence. If you feel ready, take a small step towards sharing your secret with someone you trust deeply. Notice how it feels to release the burden of secrecy and invite another person into your inner world. Alternatively, if you decide to keep your secret for now, honor your intuition and trust that the right time for disclosure will reveal itself in due course.

TRANSFORMATION/RESULTS

Remember, the power of a secret lies not in its concealment but in the mindful choice of when and with whom to share it. As you develop a clearer understanding of secrecy and trust, you will experience increased emotional resilience and empowerment.

SPRING

As we turn the last page of Winter's narrative, where we delved into the art of preparation and strategic introspection, we ready ourselves for the awakening that spring promises. We carry forward the wisdom gleaned from quiet reflection, now poised to apply it in the burgeoning world around us. This is the season of renewal, new beginnings, and the initial stages of transformation. This is the time for you to step beyond the familiar thresholds of your comfort zone and venture into new territories of personal growth. Out of your comfort zone and begin your journey of personal growth, this is your moment to plant the seeds of change and nurture them to fruition.

As the world awakens, so too should your spirit, eager to embrace the budding opportunities that unfold with each lengthening day.

Spring is your invitation to grow, to renew, and to begin anew with vigor and enthusiasm on the journey of transformation that lies ahead.

EMBRACING CHALLENGES

THE POWER OF
THE HOOK

TRANSFORMING CIRCLES FOR CHANGE

In the journey of life, I needed to find a different circle in order to experience change. Usually, it is stated that, "your circle must have a hook. If you don't have the hook then you will go round and round," and there's no end; the same information, resources, expertise, and habits will continue to go round and round. However, if your circle hooks onto another circle then the energy information, resources, expertise, habits coming out of that circle are going to flow into your circle propelling you towards your goals and aspirations.

REFLECTIVE CHALLENGE

Think back on moments in your life when you felt stuck or stagnant. Consider the circles you were a part of during those times—did they offer opportunities for growth and advancement, or were they merely repeating cycles of the same old patterns? Reflect on whether your current circles are leading you to go "round and round" without making progress. What changes can you make to avoid repetitive patterns and find fresh perspectives?

INTERACTIVE EXERCISE

Take inventory of the circles in your life and identify one circle that lacks a hook for growth and advancement. Consider ways to expand your network and connect with individuals or groups that align with your aspirations. Reach out to someone new, attend networking events, or join online communities related to your interests and goals. Brainstorm ways to connect with new circles that offer opportunities for learning, growth, and expansion. Share your insights with a trusted friend or mentor, and commit to taking proactive steps towards joining circles with hooks.

TRANSFORMATIONAL/RESULTS

As you step outside of your comfort zone and embrace new connections, notice how your circle expands and evolves, opening up new possibilities for growth and transformation both personally and professionally. Creating links between your circle and others will allow you to build a diverse network of support, enriching your life with new insights and sustainable relationships.

EMBRACING UNEXPECTED BLESSINGS

Embarking on a new chapter is like stepping into the unknown—the characters, relationships, scenery, and plot unfold gradually, revealing surprises until the final page. Nearly three decades into life, an unexpected opportunity presented itself: the chance to experience motherhood. Despite having cared for children who weren't biologically mine, this experience brought a unique blend of strength, vulnerability, and an unparalleled need to protect.

This little being, different from others I had cared for, shattered the boundaries that previous experiences had built. The fear heightened, risk-taking decreased, and the emotions of protecting and expressing love reached new heights. Life's twists and turns brought me to a juncture where motherhood took on a fresh perspective, filled with unknowns.

As I approached five decades of life, close to the anticipated empty nest and envisioning a transition into a DIVA lifestyle, life threw me an unexpected curveball. Little feet, little hands, cries, screams, and the constant refrain of "NO" precede the sweet words of "Yes" and the repeated calls of "mummy, mamma, mum." The unexpected journey of raising a child at this stage prompted questions about energy, temperament, knowledge, and strength.

This chapter takes me on a journey of continuous learning, relearning, and unlearning. In this new time, with new scenery and evolving plots, every day brings lessons and challenges. The experience unfolds, revealing nuances that were previously unknown. The chapter is a testament to the fact that understanding comes only through experience.

REFLECTIVE CHALLENGE

Reflect on the challenges and opportunities presented on one of your unexpected journeys. How has this experience changed your perspective on life's journey? Consider the lessons learned and the strength gained through the twists and turns of your unique journey.

INTERACTIVE EXERCISE

Document your experiences, thoughts, and emotions throughout this part of the journey of your life. This practice can help you process your journey and gain insights into your growth. Practice meditation, deep breathing, or other techniques to maintain a sense of calm amidst the challenges. Seek out and engage with a community of peers who share similar experiences. Share stories, challenges, and triumphs to gain different perspectives and support each other.

TRANSFORMATION/ RESULTS

Facing the unknown can be daunting. Despite uncertainties, the journey brings opportunities to grow, evolve, and discover strengths previously untapped. Be encouraged, trust the journey, and let life unfold with grace and resilience.

AVOIDING THE ZIG ZAG

Usually, when I know my days are very overwhelming with so many things to do and I can't seem to find time when I look at the tasks to be completed, I start the morning by meeting with my creator, seeking counsel and guidance on the way I should go and the things I should do for the day.

But this particular Sunday morning I decided I didn't have anything overwhelming. I didn't have many errands that I couldn't handle and therefore I will just go about my business. Interesting enough I started my errands, I started in the East then found myself going further. I would then make a circular drive returning to right back where I started to then realize I needed to go back again to collect an important item. When I reflected on the morning I recognised that there was no organization or structure. Seems like I was just moving aimlessly.

It felt like I was moving from pillar to pillar, not knowing which pillar, going back to the next pillar, and running back to the previous pillar. And then, in the middle of it all, I stopped and said to myself, "Clearly, I did not seek counsel." I **thought,** as simple as it seemed and not as overwhelming as it was, I could carry out the day's errands easily.

Have you ever had a zigzag where you have gone hither and yonder, no place to wonder because you did not acknowledge Him in all your ways and leaned unto your own understanding? As simple as a task may seem, it doesn't have to be overwhelming. Take note that we need not lean unto our own understanding but to trust in our Creator as He **will** direct our path.

What seemed realistic felt unrealistic, and if I had sought counsel, I would have been directed on how to be victorious, how to achieve, how to conquer everything I had to do in a more timely, efficient manner. And may I add, fuel-efficient as well.

I started off my drive with a full tank of gas and ended with half a tank driving a perimeter that wasn't even wide. What are you zigzagging today? Did you seek counsel or did you think it seemed easy enough to lean on your own understanding?

REFLECTIVE CHALLENGE

Take a moment to reflect on instances in your life where you've embarked on tasks without seeking guidance. How did it turn out? Were there unnecessary detours, or did the journey unfold seamlessly?

INTERACTIVE EXERCISE

Identify a current task or challenge in your life. Reflect on whether you've sought counsel or if you're leaning solely on your understanding. Share your thoughts on how seeking guidance could potentially transform the situation.

TRANSFORMATION/RESULTS

The zigzag pattern becomes a metaphor for life's challenges. Often, when we rely solely on our understanding, we find ourselves moving between pillars of confusion, uncertainty, and missed opportunities. As you navigate through life's challenges, remember that seeking counsel is not a sign of weakness but a source of strength. The simplicity of seeking counsel can be overshadowed by the illusion of self-sufficiency.

THE MARATHON OF MARRIAGE

THE THREE-LEGGED RACE PART I

To qualify for this race you must have a partner as this is a three legged race. You and your partner will be connected at the starting line before you start the race. Some take this race as a mad dash but it is a long distance race, a certain set of skills are required, a level of endurance, level of patience, level of tolerance for all the things you will encounter in this race. This is not a race for the faint of heart. Sometimes you start off great running with your partner and sometimes your partner or you may have an incident or accident, and because of that you no longer can run , crawl or walk as you started. You may have to limp until the sprain is healed, the cut is healed, or you may have to carry your partner to the finish line. No matter what, you should not leave the race, you have to make it to the finish line. Anytime you or your partner decide that you no longer want to run, walk, crawl in this race, it means that the race has ended for both of you. This is not a race only for the swiftest but for those who will endure to the end. Can you guess what race this is?

REFLECTIVE CHALLENGES

Reflect on past experiences where you faced adversity or setbacks and how you navigated through them. Next, consider the importance of compatibility, trust, and mutual support in your relationship. Reflect on past experiences with partners or teammates. Identify lessons learned and areas for growth.

INTERACTIVE EXERCISE

Share with your partner or a trusted friend specific instances where you exhibited resilience, perseverance, and determination in overcoming obstacles, whether personal, professional, or relational.

TRANSFORMATION /RESULTS

Through reflection and action, you will develop a mindset of endurance and determination, embracing the journey with your partner and staying committed to reaching the finish line together.

THE THREE-LEGGED RACE PART II

Sometimes, unfortunately, some persons try to run the race solo using their own strength and their skills even though they are tied to their partner. Consequently, their partner may be bruised, wounded on the floor but by being dragged, there is more pain, more wound to the injury. Their focus seems self-centered with no concern for their partner. Sometimes, other three-legged participants in the race may bounce into other participants, some may stop to counsel on how best to make the next move in the race or some may stop to distract you in the race, but no matter what, the race can only continue with two persons running in the race. When you have three or more persons connected to run, it becomes muddled, confused, the pace of left and right slows, and confusion increases. Some single persons try to get into the race, but it isn't that easy. They will have to meet at the starting line with the proposed partner alone and be tied to start the race. They cannot enter the race, wherever the proposed partner is, even if the other partner exits the race. This is not a relay. They can be a cheerleader on the side, they can run, walk, jog, or crawl anywhere on the side, but they can never join the race as a single person. Stay tuned for part 3 of this three-legged race and find out more about who is in it.

REFLECTIVE CHALLENGE

Reflect on times when you may have inadvertently disregarded the needs or well-being of your partner or teammate. Examine any patterns of self-centeredness or individualism that may have hindered effective partnership. Were there any potential impacts from external influences, distractions, or conflicts on your partnership dynamics?

INTERACTIVE EXERCISE

Share with a partner or trusted friend lessons learned for real-life partnerships.

TRANSFORMATION/RESULTS

Increased self-awareness will enable you to recognize and address any tendencies toward self-centeredness or individualism, fostering a greater sense of accountability toward your partner.

TRANSFORMATIONAL JOURNEYS

EMBRACING CHANGE IN LIFE'S CHAPTERS

Exploring my thoughts recently, I reflected on how the little prince and princess in my household perceive me differently. At 2¾ years old, the little prince demands affectionate gestures, while my princess, at the same age, sought expression in different ways. My 20-year-old observes these interactions, noting shifts in discipline and opportunities, expressing a sentiment I don't entirely agree with. Yet, as I pondered, I realized that they both experience me differently, shaped by the evolving chapters of my life.

The little prince has taught me the art of embracing his love language: demanding hugs, time, and affirming smiles before venturing forth. In contrast, my princess expressed herself differently at the same age. I adapt to their unique needs, navigating the nuances of their evolving personalities.

The contrast between my 20-year-old's perceptions and mine underscores the inevitable shifts in my life. My physical, spiritual, mental, and financial well-being have undergone changes, prompting new priorities and perspectives. The experiences between these two children reveal a dynamic journey where roles and approaches adjust accordingly.

Life is a series of changing faces, and people will experience you differently at various stages. The person you were in 2004 is not the person you are in 2024, and that's a testament to growth. Whether it's patience, impatience, politeness, sarcasm, randomness, or strategy, change is inevitable, reflecting the lessons learned along the way.

Recalling an elderly lady using expletives, I realize that perceptions can shift. What the little prince and princess say about me at 80-plus years, remains a mystery. Consistency is a challenge, as life's journey imparts valuable lessons. People experience your growth, adaptability, and transformation, mirroring the chapters of your life. As we evolve, so do our expressions, thoughts, and understanding.

In every moment, are people experiencing the best version of you? Be encouraged to embrace the ever-changing narrative of your life. Trust that the next chapter holds the promise of continued growth, adaptation, and the beauty that comes with evolving into the best version of yourself.

REFLECTIVE CHALLENGE

Consider the chapters of your own life as a student, an employee, a parent, a partner. How have you evolved over the years? How do others experience you now compared to earlier chapters? Reflect on the changes in your perspectives, behaviors, and priorities.

INTERACTIVE EXERCISE

Have conversations with a friend about your perspective and their perspectives in the various roles outlined in the challenge. This dialogue can offer valuable insights and help you understand how you are perceived and the impact you have on the people around you.

TRANSFORMATION/ RESULTS

Life's journey is an ever-evolving chapter. Embrace the changes, learn from the experiences, and trust that each chapter contributes to the unique story of your life. Be open to growth, adaptability, and the continuous transformation that shapes the narrative of who you are becoming.

Navigating Life's Roller Coaster

A few years ago, I took a ride on a roller coaster at a renowned theme park. The three-minute thrill felt like an eternity, with unexpected twists and turns that heightened the experience. Little did I know, a similar roller coaster awaited me in a particular chapter of my life – a chapter I aptly named the "Running Chapter."

Much like the roller coaster ride, the issues in this chapter of my life seemed to persistently cross over into others. The antagonist, an unexpected character, would vanish only to reappear, creating a plot thick with uncertainty. The intricacies of this particular chapter became apparent only when securely seated, and the ride commenced.

Continued anxiety and palpitations from this ongoing chapter began to impact not only the characters directly involved but overflowed into other aspects of my life. The realization struck that this turbulent chapter needed closure. Despite the highest level of interest from all parties involved, I understood that the battle was not solely mine to fight.

With a commitment to closure and the highest stakes in mind, a decision was made to bring an end to this tumultuous chapter. The battles, the lessons learned, and the invaluable insights gained had reached their culmination. The narrative of this chapter concluded, allowing for healing and closure.

Encountering antagonists in life is inevitable. Learning valuable lessons from their presence, identifying boundaries, and controlling what is within one's power are key aspects of navigating such challenges. The roller coaster ride of this chapter, with its ups and downs, had to come to an end.

As the chapter concluded, it became essential to take note of the feelings and disposition that remained. These defining moments would shape how I engaged with future antagonists, ensuring a more resilient and empowered approach to life's challenges.

Life is a series of chapters, each with its own challenges and lessons. Be encouraged to trust the next chapter of your life. Anticipate the unexpected, learn from the roller-coaster rides, and use the experiences gained to navigate future challenges with resilience and wisdom.

REFLECTIVE CHALLENGE

Reflect on your own life's roller coaster rides. What chapters have felt like a turbulent journey? How did you navigate them, and what lessons did you carry forward?

INTERACTIVE EXERCISES

Write a letter of closure to the antagonist in your chapter, releasing physical or emotional mementos associated with the chapter. This exercise will allow you to embrace healing and closure, paving the way for new beginnings.

TRANSFORMATION/RESULTS

The "running chapter" of life, much like a roller coaster, has its twists and turns. The decision to bring closure marked a significant step towards healing and growth. As you face your own challenges, trust that each chapter, no matter how turbulent, contributes to your journey. Embrace the lessons, reinforce your boundaries, find closure when necessary, and trust the next chapter that awaits.

FROM THE BACK ROWS TO THE FRONT

A JOURNEY OF GUIDANCE AND TRANSFORMATION

In the realm of **aerobics, every step** is a metaphor for life's journey. As I **stepped into** that aerobics class for the first time, I **remembered** that I was not just there to work out but to embark on a transformative journey. I considered that as I advance in life, others are looking to me for guidance. The aerobics class is a microcosm of this journey, where our initial struggle is not a weakness but a stepping stone toward something greater. It's interesting how, at the beginning, we might find ourselves struggling to keep up for the first 45 minutes to an hour. The parallels with life are striking—the initial challenges, the moments of self-doubt. Yet, with time, our endurance increases, and our resistance strengthens. We move from the rows at the back to the rows up front, symbolizing a personal evolution.

Now, we are not just participants; we have become a model in front. Those behind us are looking to us for guidance, watching our every move to keep up with their steps.

You've become the beacon that others rely on to navigate the dance of life.

Having been at the back, we understand the significance of our role. Our journey becomes more than a personal accomplishment; it's a responsibility to those still finding their way. Those at the back count on us, not just to keep up but to guide them through this dance of life.

REFLECTIVE CHALLENGE

Pause for a moment. Consider your own journey—the challenges you've faced, the moments of triumph, and the people who guided you. Write down three key lessons you've learned along your path. What transformations have you experienced, and who might be silently looking up to you?

INTERACTIVE EXERCISE:

How do you feel about being a guide for others? Discuss a time when you struggled in life on an issue and how you overcame it. How did this experience shape your perspective on challenges in life? Share your insights with a trusted friend or mentor, and commit to making a conscious effort in the decisions before acting upon them.

TRANSFORMATION/ RESULTS

In life's aerobics class, we all start somewhere—sometimes at the back. But as we move forward, there are those who will follow in our footsteps. It's a continuous cycle of guidance, transformation, and the uplifting rhythm of life.

As you move from the back to the front, reflect on the invisible audience you're guiding unknowingly. Who is looking at you for inspiration, for guidance? Your journey has a ripple effect, touching lives you may not even be aware of.

UNVEILING THE UNSEEN

A CHALLENGE TO HIKE YOUR OWN TERRAIN

Embark on a journey through terrains that others shy away from: I challenge you.

As an avid hiker, I experienced the most serene, beautiful, peaceful and barely touched places that were always well hidden away. I would only experience their beauty after long, tedious and sometimes dangerous terrain that winded with straits, valleys and hills, but when I arrived there only few would have visited and I would have the opportunity to uncover such a beauty.

The easier the hike the more persons visited the space, and after a while, it became not as beautiful as it once was, not as serene as it once was, not as peaceful as it once was because it had just become a normal space . For me the prize would have only been received when I was committed to the terrain through the sweat, the groans and the aching muscles. I had the opportunity to notice the beauty and observe the dangers but I didn't turn back. My challenge was to hike through the terrain that no one else wanted to journey, to do the things that no one else wanted to do, to the achieve the things that no one else would achieve.

I challenged myself to be the first or the first in a few to uncover the things that were untouched and to experience the beauty, the Serenity, the peace and win the prize.

I challenge you to hike through your terrain, that journey no one else wants to do, to achieve the things that no one else will achieve. I challenge you to be the first or be among a few to uncover the things that are untouched and experience the beauty, the serenity, the peace and win the prize.

REFLECTIVE CHALLENGE

Reflect on an aspect of your life where you have been hesitant to take a new path. Consider a project or a current challenge in your life you have been putting off because of the difficulty involved. Reflect and list the potential rewards that lie in exploring this uncharted territory. Challenge yourself to step out of your comfort zone and pursue this journey, even if others avoid it.

INTERACTIVE EXERCISE:

Share with a friend a personal story about a time you took a risk in your life and what you learned from it. List all the things you wish to uncover in your life.

TRANSFORMATION/ RESULTS

By embracing the unknown, you will discover hidden strengths within yourself and uncover new opportunities that others may never experience. Perseverance through challenges will not only lead you to serene and beautiful places, but it will also bring you a deep sense of accomplishment and inner peace.

In the challenge to hike through the terrain that no one else wants to traverse lies the opportunity for transformation, discovery, and the winning of a prize that is uniquely yours. I challenge you to embrace the path less traveled and unveil the unseen wonders that await you.

RIDING THROUGH CHALLENGES

Observing my 2½-year-old navigate his tricycle fearlessly sparked memories of my own bicycle journey. Unlike my siblings, I always had the support of my father guiding me. This reflection reminded me of a pivotal moment when I decided to conquer my fear of riding alone, revealing the powerful role of the mind in overcoming challenges.

While my siblings rode freely, I relied on my father's support, whether holding the handles or guiding the rear of the bicycle. His presence provided a safety net, allowing me to ride without fear. This support, however, had its limits.

At the age of 10, faced with a new BMX bike and a neighborhood pact to ride together on Christmas, I realized my father couldn't accompany me throughout the neighborhood. Determined not to be left behind, I took matters into my own hands. The challenge was daunting, but the desire to keep up with the group outweighed the fear of failure.

With each fall, I got back up, pedaled past the gravel heap, and repeated the process. The fear of being left behind fueled my determination. By the afternoon, I had conquered the basics and joined the group for the neighborhood ride.

REFLECTIVE CHALLENGE

In this moment, pause and reflect on your own childhood challenges. What fears did you face, and how did you overcome them? Consider the early lessons that shaped your understanding of persistence and determination.

INTERACTIVE EXERCISE

Take a moment to connect this lesson to your current challenges. What obstacles are you facing, and how can the power of your mind guide you through? Consider the possibilities within yourself. Connect with a supportive friend, family member, or mentor who can serve as your bicycle buddy throughout your journey of personal growth and transformation. Share your fears, goals, and progress with your bicycle buddy, fostering accountability and encouragement. Celebrate the milestones.

TRANSFORMATION/ RESULTS

As you face challenges, consider the bicycle you're trying to ride today. Recognize your resources, set clear goals, and tap into the power of your mind. With practice, persistence, and a focused mind, one can achieve anything. The Bible's affirmation, "I can do all things through Christ who strengthens me" (Philippians 4:13), emphasizes the limitless potential within us. You have the capability to overcome, achieve, and ride through any challenge.

THE JOURNEY OF RELEASING INVESTMENTS

Prior to two decades ago, I would have experienced loss, and then during the last decade or so I would have again experienced that type of loss a number of times. It's something that happens, but it's usually kept very silent or very rarely spoken of because it's like a taboo. We don't want to speak about miscarriages. I've had the experience of carrying up to a particular length of time and then losing that pregnancy. But over two decades ago I had the opportunity, even through a threatened miscarriage, to give birth, to experience birth, to experience becoming a biological mother.

After over two decades, I released what I was given the opportunity to be a steward for. I released it into a space of its own. She is on her journey, a journey that God has already mapped out for her before she was even birthed, a journey that requires a relationship with God to make it easier and more peaceful. A journey that, even though you make decisions that are not in His favor, God will never forsake or leave you. Because one thing he gives us is choice. Today I release her on her journey. I would have given her a tool box . Difficult as it felt during this week I had a number of mixed feelings. Some of uncertainty, some that required patience some that even felt like a little bit of fear but I had to go back to 'he did not give me a spirit of fear, but of power and of love and of sound mind and I had to return to the promise that all my children will be taught by the Lord and they will be prosperous in peace. So he called her, he would choose her and he will guide her in the way she should go and just like I found him she will find him and today I released what I was blessed with over 2 decades ago to be on her journey, my princess. Watching on from the sideline, praying from the sideline, covering her from the side line as much as I could ,but allowing her to run her race to pull her toolbox, to focus on whoever is in front of her that is hopefully going in the right direction and to build her relationship with God.

REFLECTIVE CHALLENGE

Reflect on experiences of loss and the emotions associated with them. Explore how you typically cope with mixed emotions and navigate through challenging times.

INTERACTIVE EXERCISE

Close your eyes and visualize a toolbox filled with tools representing qualities or resources that support you during challenging times.

Reflect on each tool and its significance, such as courage, resilience, love, and faith. Identify which tools you already possess and which ones you may need to cultivate or strengthen.

TRANSFORMATION /RESULTS

You will engage in a process of emotional healing and self-discovery. Developing a deeper understanding of your emotions will allow you to navigate through grief, uncertainty, and fear with greater resilience and self-compassion.

Embrace the concept of release as a catalyst for personal growth and transformation, allowing you to move forward with confidence and intention.

THE POWER OF WHY

Crawling out of bed early in the morning to shift to another space within the house felt familiar, but this particular morning demanded more. Exiting the comfort of my home was a challenge, especially on a public holiday when the allure of extra sleep was tempting. My trainer had invited me for a morning session, disrupting my preferred afternoon routine.

Despite my reluctance, the chapter I'm currently navigating demands a heightened commitment. A mission-driven focus propelled me out of bed, dressed, and mentally prepared for the challenges that awaited me, even in the chilly morning air. The why became my anchor, pushing me beyond my comfort zone.

Arriving at the training space, my gaze fell upon the set-up – tires, ropes, weights – and the internal dialogue started. The thought of getting it over with lingered, but the process unfolded. It required pulling out efforts I didn't initially feel like exerting, all while keeping focus on the underlying why that fueled this chapter of my life.

As the exercise regime commenced, a quarter-mile run for each round became a pivotal challenge. Slowing from a run to a crawl, the difficulty became apparent. To navigate this physical and mental struggle, I sought deeper inspiration. Music became the catalyst, transforming my pace from a crawl back to a run, focusing on the tunes rather than the fatigue and leg pain.

The morning routine felt tougher than my accustomed evening sessions. The struggle wasn't just against the physical challenges but also the different atmosphere, a body transitioning from a night's fast, and a mind still in rest mode. Every element was distinct in the morning, except for the unwavering presence of the Trainer.

By the fourth round, the battle intensified, and my pace evolved into a crawl. Digging deep for sets and reps, I tapped into the profound reminder of why. The morning session, despite its initially unwelcome nature, became a testament to the transformative power of a compelling purpose.

REFLECTIVE CHALLENGE

Reflect on moments when you faced challenges in the morning. What motivated you to push through? Consider the power of purpose in those instances.

INTERACTIVE EXERCISE

Write down your "why" - the compelling purpose that drives you to overcome obstacles and pursue your goals. Share it with a trusted friend or family member and discuss how it resonates with them.

TRANSFORMATION/ RESULTS

For those facing challenges, be it in fitness or life, acknowledge the resistance but keep the "why" in focus. Embrace discomfort, seek inspiration, and let the power of purpose propel you forward. Know that every crawl, every struggle, is a step closer to the end goal.

SUMMER

With the close ofspring,, where we embraced new beginnings and ventured beyond familiar borders, we find ourselves at the threshold of summer—aa season of heightened action and perseverance. The challenges we chose to confront have prepared us, like a river smoothing stones, for the vigorous currents of summer. This next chapter is one of vibrant engagement, where our resilience is tested under the long stretch of the sun's rays. As the sun climbs high and fills the days with light, you are called to engage fully with the challenges and opportunities that come your way. This is the time to embrace the energy of your ongoing transformation, to push forward with heat and heart alike.

In the midst of summer's intensity, you are encouraged to remain resilient, to water the seeds of spring's ambitions with sweat and determination. Trust the journey you are on, knowing that each step taken in the summer's glow is a step towards realizing your potential. Let the long days be your ally as you persist, and let the warm nights reward you with rest and reflection on all you have achieved. Summer is your time to thrive, to harness the full power of your transformation, and to see just how far your efforts can take you.

PERSISTENCE AND RESILIENCE

BUILDING RESILIENCE IN THE HOME

In the serene embrace of our rural neighborhood, my husband and I embarked on a transformative journey to craft our dream home. With each hammer strike and beam placement, our optimism soared, fueled by the vision of our ideal sanctuary. However, as fate would have it, our dream encountered an unexpected pause—a financial hiccup that halted the completion of our sanctuary, leaving a portion exposed to the elements.

As the winds of uncertainty swept through our unfinished structure, it became a poignant reflection of life's unpredictable nature. The wide beams and exposed steel served as mirrors, revealing not just infrastructural challenges but also the hidden complexities within our family dynamics. In the face of this dilemma, we were compelled to pause and reflect.

Amidst the chaos, we found clarity. The exposure brought about by external forces acted as a catalyst, laying bare the vulnerabilities that required reinforcement. It was a pivotal moment—a call to strengthen the foundation, both literally and metaphorically.

We made the conscious decision to invest in the reinforcement process, knowing full well that it would not be swift or inexpensive. Yet, we recognized the intrinsic value of this investment. As we drew parallels between the physical structure of our home and the intangible bonds of our relationships, profound realizations emerged.

We learned that, much like infrastructure, relationships require exposure to external elements to unveil their shortcomings. Quick fixes may offer temporary relief, but true strength lies in addressing the underlying issues with patience and intentionality. It was a lesson in resilience—a testament to the enduring power of vulnerability and perseverance.

Through the process of reinforcement, our journey transformed into a tale of growth and resilience. We embraced the storms, weathering each challenge with unwavering determination. And in the end, we didn't just build a house; we constructed a resilient home—a sanctuary that stood strong against the tests of time and adversity.

REFLECTIVE CHALLENGE

Pause for a moment and reflect on the unfinished structures in your own life. What vulnerabilities and challenges do they reveal? Consider how these moments of exposure can serve as opportunities for growth and reinforcement in your relationships and endeavors.

INTERACTIVE EXERCISE

Identify one area of your life or relationship that feels unfinished or vulnerable. Explore ways in which you can invest in reinforcement and resilience, whether through open communication, seeking professional guidance, or fostering a spirit of resilience and perseverance. Share your insights with a trusted friend or loved one, and together, embark on a journey of growth and transformation.

TRANSFORMATION/ RESULTS

So, as you navigate the construction of your lives and relationships, don't shy away from the exposed truths. Embrace the storms, reinforce what needs strengthening, and build a foundation that withstands the test of time. After all, the true measure of control is in your ability to shape something not just aesthetically pleasing but enduringly strong within.

ONE MORE FOR BAD MIND
PERSISTENCE AND TRANSFORMATION

In the early 2000s, post-pregnancy, a realization dawned—I had accumulated excess weight, and the echoes of sluggishness reverberated. The desire to be toned stirred within me, prompting a journey to the gym. Despite a distaste for cardio exercises, I committed to the pursuit of transformation.

Weight training became my preferred avenue at the gym, a pathway to reshape my body and overcome the challenges of cardio exercises. The regimen was demanding—legs, uppers, total body—with repetitions ranging from 20 to 25. It was a grueling process, but the weights changed, and so did my determination. In moments of physical exhaus-tion, when sweat dripped and muscles screamed, a remarkable lesson unfolded. My trainer, recognizing my struggle, would intervene with the words, "Give me one more for bad mind." His words ignited a spark within me. The mental shift allowed me to transcend physical boundaries, pushing beyond what seemed impossible. The pursuit of a goal, the dream etched vividly in your mind, can be challenging. When it feels like you've given your all—time, finances, heart—and disappointment creeps in, remember the mantra. **Don't give up; give it one more for bad mind**. The mind governs every step, every effort. That one extra push can redefine your journey. The persistence paid off. "One more for bad mind" became a catalyst for transformation. A year later, the results were astounding—several dress sizes dropped, a more toned physique, and newfound strength. The lesson was clear: giving it one more, especially when it seemed impossible, had a transformative impact.

REFLECTIVE CHALLENGE

Pause and reflect on your journey from where you started to where you are now. Consider how you have grown and transformed, not just physically but also mentally and emotionally. Reflect on areas of your life where you might be avoiding discomfort. List these areas. Challenge yourself to embrace the difficult aspects of your journey, as they can lead to growth. Consider the power of "one more" for bad mind. Where can you summon that extra effort, that additional push to break through barriers?

INTERACTIVE EXERCISE

Create a personal mantra to motivate yourself when you face challenges. Share this mantra with a mentor or friend for accountability. Use this mantra as a mental tool to push yourself beyond your perceived limits.

TRANSFORMATION/ RESULTS.

In the journey of physical transformation, the mantra "One more for bad mind" became a guiding force. Apply this mindset to your aspirations, your goals, and witness the transformative power of persistence. Don't give up; give it one more for bad mind, and watch your dreams reshape into reality. By pushing beyond your perceived limits and embracing challenges, you will transform not just your body, but your mindset and resilience.

TRUSTING THE PROCESS

TRUSTING THE PROCESS

A CATERPILLAR'S JOURNEY TO TRANSFORMATION

L et me share a story that reflects the start of my journey.

In a quiet garden, amidst the whispers of the wind and the rustle of leaves, a curious caterpillar named Pet resided. His world, bound by the earth and the branches of a coconut tree, seemed ordinary and unchanging. Yet, every day, he awaited the arrival of his dear friend Butter, the butterfly, whose tales of adventure and wonder ignited a spark of curiosity within him.

Butter, with her vibrant orange wings and tales of distant lands, was a source of inspiration for Pet. Though confined to his earthly existence, he longed to experience the world beyond the confines of his cocoon. Little did he know that change was already stirring within him, a transformation waiting to unfold.

REFLECTIVE CHALLENGE

Reflect on your dreams and aspirations. Are there aspects of your life you wish to explore more deeply? Challenge yourself to embrace the unknown and consider what changes may be stirring within you. How can you take steps to expand your horizons?

INTERACTIVE EXERCISE

Write a letter to your future self, imagining the changes you hope to undergo and the adventures you want to experience. This can help you set intentions for your own transformation.

TRANSFORMATION/ RESULTS

By embracing your curiosity and seeking new experiences, you will open yourself to transformation and growth beyond your previous limitations. Through the guidance and inspiration of those around you, welcome change and allow yourself to evolve. You will discover new paths and embark on a journey of self-discovery and transformation.

THE UNCERTAINTY IN TRANSFORMATION

One day, Pet confided in Butter, expressing the strange sensation he felt inside. "Butter, I feel a flutter of wings and a sense of change within me," Pet said, his voice tinged with uncertainty. Butter, with her serene demeanor, reassured him, "Trust the process, my friend. Change is the path to becoming who you are meant to be."

The next day, when Butter visited, she called out for Pet, who was hiding away in a dark brown cocoon. "Pet, Pet!" she called, her voice echoing through the garden. From within the cocoon, Pet answered, "Butter, I am here. I don't know what is happening to me. I feel different, and my head hurts. I am scared." Butter's comforting words reached him, "Trust the process, Pet. Embrace the transformation."

Butter visited Pet every day, sharing her stories and ending each visit with the same gentle encouragement: "Trust the process." Pet found solace in her words, though he still struggled with the uncertainty of his journey.

Then one day, during Butter's visit, Pet grew quiet. His cocoon began to tremble, signaling the culmination of his transformation. Butter hovered above, taking in the view as the cocoon cracked open. A bright orange and yellow butterfly slowly emerged, wing by wing. Pet, now transformed, looked relieved.

Butter flew closer to her friend, her eyes filled with pride and joy. "You made it, my friend," she said with warmth. Together, they flapped their wings, taking flight and whispering in unison, "Trust the process." As they soared through the garden, Pet embraced his new life as a butterfly, ready to embark on his own adventures alongside his dear friend Butter. Together, they explored new horizons, their wings carrying them toward a world of endless stories and discoveries.

REFLECTIVE CHALLENGE

I challenge you to pause for a moment and reflect on your own journey of life. Consider a time when you felt uncertainty. How did you handle that moment, and what lessons did you learn from it? What steps did you take to embrace the change? How did this moment shape the person you are today?

INTERACTIVE EXERCISE

Write a gratitude letter to someone who has supported you during a time of change. This exercise can help you express appreciation and acknowledge the role of others in your transformation.

TRANSFORMATION/RESULTS

By embracing change and trusting the process, you will emerge stronger and more resilient, ready to embark on new adventures and explore new horizons. Through facing uncertainty and challenges, you will learn to embrace the journey. Celebrate the process and the outcomes as you embark on new experiences with confidence and joy.

THE THREE-LEGGED RACE PART III

In 2008, I entered this race, sure that I was guided by the Lord. A decade and a half later, with laughter, tears, injuries, and healing, my partner and I are still in this race. The criterion to enter this race is that you had to have a spouse.

There is a biblical saying, "What God has joined together let no man separate." You see, when you decide to join this race you and your partner are joined with a cord that cannot be broken. Are you willing to run this race, walk this race or be in this race? If you are, be prepared. It is not a 100m dash; it's long distance. It will take time to hydrate ever so often, to slow down so often, and reflect on why you are in this race because you are not running this race alone. This race will teach you endurance, tolerance, patience, and, most importantly, love. There is an old African proverb which says, "If you want to go fast, go alone, but if you want to go far, you need to go together." Remember, this is a three-legged race. Are you cheerleading, running, walking, jogging, or crawling on the side, or are you in this race? Which race are you in?

REFLECTIVE EXERCISE

Reflect on your commitment to your partner and the endurance required to navigate the challenges of long-term relationships. Consider the reasons why you entered into this partnership and the values that sustain you both through the ups and downs of the journey.

INTERACTIVE EXERCISE

Write a heartfelt letter or message to your partner, expressing your feelings and reflecting on cherished memories shared together.

TRANSFORMATION/RESULTS

Personal commitment and relationship dynamics renew your commitment to the partnership and build resilience in navigating challenges. Through reflection and introspection, you will gain clarity on your role within the relationship and commit to nurturing and sustaining your partnership for the long haul.

UNDERSTANDING THE "BIGGER PICTURE"

In my experience with partnerships, my former companion often urged me to see the bigger picture whenever disagreements arose. I firmly believe that we are all integral pieces of a larger mosaic, each possessing a unique contribution. However, my struggle lay in perceiving this grand composition amid what seemed like a chaotic blend of colors and forms.

To my partner's plea for a broader perspective, I confessed my difficulty. The bigger picture appeared to me like a mural obscured by splash art—beautiful yet unclear. Clarity was the key; I yearned for a lucid understanding of the larger canvas to contribute effectively—armed with the right resources, temperament, and timing.

Our paths eventually diverged, a consequence of my perpetual challenge in grasping the bigger picture. The separation underscored my inability to feel aligned with the grand opportunity that lay ahead. Yet, it prompted a profound realization about the importance of shared visions in relationships.

Whether in business partnerships or personal connections, navigating the intricacies of the bigger picture is paramount. Knowing where you are headed, understanding your collective destination, and defining your role in the broader context are crucial. A lack of clarity in contribution can lead to disagreement.

REFLECTIVE CHALLENGE

Pause and reflect on your own relationships. Do you and your partner share a common vision of the bigger picture? How do you define the bigger picture for yourself and with others? What are your individual and collective destinations? Are your contributions aligned with the overarching goals? Assess whether you both see the same canvas and whether your actions are harmonizing towards the same masterpiece.

INTERACTIVE EXERCISE

Organize a session with your partner(s) to discuss your collective goals, values, and aspirations, and how each person contributes to the overall vision. Each person should identify their strengths and areas of expertise. This helps define clear roles and responsibilities in the partnership, promoting a better understanding of how each person contributes.

TRANSFORMATION/RESULTS

In the masterpiece of relationships, perceiving the bigger picture is a shared responsibility. It is not merely about seeing but understanding, contributing, and aligning actions with a collective vision. The beauty lies in the harmony of contributions, creating a masterpiece that transcends the individual strokes. Reevaluate, realign, and ensure that you and your partner are both contributing to the canvas of the bigger picture you wish to paint together. Understanding each other's unique strengths will allow you to contribute more effectively to the larger masterpiece.

EMBRACING THE UNKNOWN IN LIFE'S JOURNEY

Today marked a crucial step in conquering a fear, both mentally and physically, to embark on a project and ensure the best possible experience. This journey unfolded with steep inclines, declines, and unexpected twists, demanding the courage to power through and overcome the unknown.

The path I chose was unfamiliar, filled with inclines and declines, symbolic of life's unpredictable journey. My desire for the experience propelled me forward, pushing me to confront fears that threatened to hold me back. To navigate this unfamiliar terrain, I sought the guidance of those who had trodden this path before, one of them being my co-pilot.

As we journeyed, seeking guidance on what lay ahead, the response from my co-pilot was simple yet profound: "Just keep driving; you will make it." The reassurance echoed in my mind, a reminder that sometimes the uncertainties in life demand a forward motion, a persistence that leads to triumph.

Amidst the inclines, there were moments when doubts crept in. The vehicle seemed to struggle, and I felt the need to press harder on the gas. Just when it felt like the vehicle might give up, the terrain shifted to a flat or a decline, providing a comfortable space to maneuver and relax. Each challenging moment was a precursor to a rewarding experience.

Life's journey is unpredictable, and the experiences are often unique to each individual. Going through something similar to others doesn't guarantee an identical experience, and there are aspects of your journey that are exclusively yours. Embracing the unknown and pressing forward becomes an intrinsic part of the personal narrative.

REFLECTIVE CHALLENGE

Take a moment to reflect on your own journey. What challenges have you faced? How have you navigated the,"hills and the valleys," Consider the times when pressing the brakes or powering up became necessary for your journey.

INTERACTIVE EXERCISE

Write a letter to your future self, reflecting on the journey and your accomplishments. This can serve as a reminder of your courage and perseverance when facing future challenges.

TRANSFORMATION/RESULTS

Wherever you find yourself on your journey—whether climbing steep inclines, descending declines, or cruising on flat terrains—there will be moments when you need to power up or mash the brakes. In those crucial minutes, when control requires braking or the ascent demands extra power, don't stop moving. Trust that every challenge, every press of the brakes, and every power-up is leading you toward a beautiful destination. Life's chapters are filled with uncertainties, but the resilience to keep moving forward ensures that the next chapter holds the promise of new experiences and triumphs.

THE HARVESTING TRANSFORMATION

Do you like picking your food fresh from a garden? I remember going to this orchard to pick oranges. Acres and acres of property with thousands of citrus plants. On the 1st occasion my husband and I started our journey before the sun rose, we were not too sure where the venue was, but we were determined to find the place. On arriving we met the owner who gave us a tip. He said, 'the Orange trees on this side here are very sweet'. Now at this orchard, you could eat as much as you wanted but whatever you wanted to carry you had to pay for. There were different varieties of orange trees. The only thing with this orchard is that it was open only for less than six hours to the public.

As it was our first time and we had only two hours left before closing we went exactly where the owner recommended. There were over a dozen trees in the area. The oranges looked healthy, and were indeed very sweet but we were only able to pick on three trees. Not one Orange on those three trees and that part of the orchard wasn't sweet.

. . .

THE NEXT SEASON we were sure to return and to the same spot because we were already familiar with. Three years later we've back and stayed in the space. This time the oranges were not as sweet as they use to be. We had to find a new spot. Sometimes you have to adapt. You have to change. If you do not either your clients will end up with poorer quality or you will move to maintain the quality you have. If what you are offering is no longer the same and your clients are changing, then you have to adapt.

REFLECTIVE CHALLENGES

Consider situations in your own life or work where you've had to balance between maintaining quality and consistency. Reflect on the trade-offs involved in prioritizing one over the other, and how you've managed similar situations in the past.

INTERACTIVE EXERCISE

Identify your target audience or client based on their specific needs or preferences. That client can be a partner, workmates, or a family member. Next, brainstorm ways to adapt your product or service to better meet these needs.

TRANSFORMATION/RESULTS

Reflect on the lessons from the orchard, recognizing the transformative power of adaptation. Embrace change as an opportunity for growth, maintaining the sweetness in various aspects of your life. By prioritizing the needs of your client and demonstrating flexibility in adapting your offerings, client's build stronger, more meaningful relationships with your customer base. You will learn to anticipate and respond to changing client preferences, fostering loyalty and trust in your brand or services.

TRANSPLANT OR BE TRANSPLANTED

My feet had just hit the floor from off my bed when my phone rang. Usually, I don't take calls or address messages before meeting with my Creator, but this particular morning I took the call, which disturbed me not because of the caller on the other end but what initiated the call.

Internalizing the situation, I considered the words, 'transplant or be transplanted'. You see, when you have a small plant and as it grows you place it in bigger pots so that the plant is able to push its roots deeper and extend its branches wider but when you don't transplant that plant it is forced to push as far as it could sometimes damaging the pot that it is in.

As individuals, sometimes we have outgrown a space, an organization, or a relationship. Instead of transplanting ourselves or allowing ourselves to be transplanted we decide to stay because of familiarity or fear of change and we try to push further causing friction and injuring emotions with those around us.

Now, if we took the opportunity to either transplant or be transplanted we would experience wider spaces, build new relationships, and enjoy the opportunity to grow better and come to our true being. But when we stay in a space which we have already outgrown, what we do is stifle our own growth.

If you look at plants that have outgrown their pots or their spaces, no matter how big they grow, they do not look as healthy even though they are pushing through the pot. Sometimes it's important for us to realize that we have outgrown our space and need to now transplant or be transplanted to another space where we can dig deeper, grow wider, and become more beautiful, coming into the being that we are supposed to be.

Remember, not all plants are made for a particular pot. Sometimes, no matter how large the pot, we have to be transplanted into the earth itself in order to reach as far as we are designed to be.

REFLECTIVE CHALLENGE

Reflect on your current space in life, including your job, relationships, and personal environment. Consider whether you have outgrown any of these spaces. Explore your fear of change and its impact on your willingness to embrace new opportunities. Reflect on past experiences where fear of change may have hindered your growth and consider how you can overcome this fear to facilitate personal transformation.

INTERACTIVE EXERCISE

Challenge yourself to expand your social and professional networks by connecting with individuals outside your current circle. Attend networking events, join online communities, and initiate conversations with people who inspire you to pursue new opportunities.

TRANSFORMATION/RESULTS

Build resilience and confidence to embrace change and seek new opportunities for growth and expansion. Overcome fear of change by recognizing the potential for personal development and fulfillment that comes with being transplanted.

THE ROLLER COASTER RIDE OF LIFE

SECURE, EXPERIENCE AND TRUST

In a previous story, I recounted the first time I experienced a roller coaster ride at a famous theme park with my daughter, niece, and nephew. The ride was a whirlwind of dips, turns, climbs, and level spaces that left lasting impressions. The parallels between this exhilarating ride and life's challenges are profound.

As the roller coaster ride began, it started slow on what seemed like a level space. However, the speed quickly intensified, and I found myself navigating through twists and turns, feeling the dips and climbs. A sense of lack of control permeated the experience. Unable to turn back or climb out, I had to endure the ride until its end. In those three minutes, I screamed, held my breath, closed my eyes, and clung to the safety bar.

Life, akin to the roller coaster rides we willingly sign up for, such as careers, parenting, and relationships, can present unexpected twists, turns, climbs, and moments of relative calm. The key, similar to the theme park ride, lies in ensuring you are securely seated before embarking on the journey. Secure your valuables, remember to breathe, scream if needed, close your eyes if necessary, and hold on tight. Acknowledge that, like the roller coaster ride, the journey will eventually come to an end.

Reflecting on the roller coaster experience with my daughter, niece, and nephew, each of us had a distinct encounter. One wanted a second round, while others were eager to explore bigger, longer rides. Much like life, people go through similar roller-coaster moments in parenting, relationships, and careers, emerging with diverse experiences shaped by their unique journeys.

Drawing a parallel between the theme park ride and life, our Creator is the attendant ensuring we are securely seated before the ride commences. If, by chance, we neglect to let Him secure us, there is assurance in knowing that the roller coaster has been maintained and is controlled by the Creator—a source of safety in life's tumultuous journey.

Just as everyone on the theme park ride had different experiences, individuals traversing the roller coaster of life will finish with distinct perspectives. Acknowledge your experience, reflect on the journey, and learn from the twists and turns.

REFLECTIVE CHALLENGE

Reflect on your own life's roller coaster rides. How have you approached the dips, turns, and climbs? What lessons have you learned, and how have these experiences shaped your unique journey?

INTERACTIVE EXERCISE

Imagine yourself on a roller coaster ride, symbolizing your journey through life's challenges. Visualize the twists, turns, and climbs, as well as moments of calm and exhilaration. Say one of the following affirmations seven (7) times.

1. I am strong, capable, and resilient. I trust in my ability to navigate life's challenges with courage and grace.
2. I am supported and surrounded by love. I lean on my support system and draw strength from their encouragement.
3. I am worthy of peace and happiness. I release

fear and embrace each moment with confidence and optimism.

4. I am guided by divine wisdom and intuition. I trust in the path set before me and surrender to the flow of life's journey.

TRANSFORMATION/RESULTS

Life's roller coaster ride, **much like the** theme park adventure, is a journey of twists and turns. As you navigate the unexpected, secure yourself, breathe through the challenges, and trust that, with the guidance of the Creator, every dip and climb contributes to the rich tapestry of your unique life story. You will gain a new perspective on your challenges and setbacks. Learn to embrace life's uncertainties as opportunities for growth and transformation, viewing each twist and turn as a chance to learn and evolve.

FALL

As summer's vibrant chapter wanes, marked by our steadfast engagement and the resilience we've shown in the face of adversity, we transition to the reflective season of fall. The efforts we've exerted and the perseverance we've demonstrated begin to yield their harvest, allowing us to reap the profound rewards of hard work. Fall invites us to slow our pace and reflect on the legacies we are crafting and the wisdom we hope to pass on. It's a time to celebrate the harvest of our personal and professional growth, preparing to share the bounty with others. The fruits of your labor come into full view, ripe for the picking. As the leaves turn and the air cools, this time beckons you to slow down, reflect, and harvest the rewards of your hard work. It's a period for savoring the satisfaction of tasks completed and challenges overcome, providing a profound sense of closure and fulfillment.

During this season, your thoughts might turn toward the legacy you are building. What lessons have you learned that you can pass on? How has your journey shaped the wisdom you will share? Fall emphasizes the importance of continuous learning—not just for your own growth but for the enrichment of others who may follow in your footsteps.

This season invites you to gather your experiences like fallen leaves, to study their colors and textures, and to prepare for the cycle to begin anew. Fall is your time to reflect on what has been and to prepare for what is yet to come, ensuring that the knowledge and insights gained are preserved and passed on, enriching not just your life but the lives of others around you.

LEGACY AND LIFELONG LEARNING

BUILDING A LEGACY

In the echoes of my father's stern words, "Every generation must be better," I now realize the depth of wisdom embedded in that simple yet profound statement. As a child, I may have interpreted it as a reprimand, but with the clarity of hindsight, I see it as a call to action—a call to transcend the limitations of the past and pave the way for a brighter future.

I had the privilege recently to celebrate a generation of my family, all over six decades. With all the pain, uncertainty, and trauma that generation would have experienced, it was notable that the generations after them had grown.

This generation lost their mother, my grandmother, before she scored 45 and their father though providing financially, seemed absent emotionally. So many factors contributed to their growth, their connectivity, and to the growth of their children.

We had to appreciate that we were standing on their shoulders and they were standing on someone else's shoulders. Though not perfect, their history has captured the why and who they have become, just like ours has and the next generation will.

I have always believed that every generation must be better than the generation before. Similarly, the generation after my generation has also achieved much more than our generation thus far, academically, spiritually, and financially.

Today, I celebrated because, through the grief, pains—physical, mental, financial—and any uncertainty, there was growth. We are standing on the shoulders of the generation before, and their grandchildren are standing on our shoulders.

I want to remind you today that you are standing on someone's shoulders. Whether it is or was stable or strong, you are standing on it. How will your shoulder be for the next generation? Every generation needs a foundation. Will you provide your shoulder willingly?

REFLECTIVE CHALLENGE

Write down three key values or principles passed down to you by previous generations. Consider your parents, grandparents, and ancestors and how their experiences, both positive and negative, have shaped your values and decisions. Consider the sacrifices made by your parents or grandparents to provide you with opportunities for growth and advancement. Reflect on the responsibility you hold as part of the generational chain. How can you ensure that your contributions pave the way for a stronger foundation for future generations? How have their investments in your education and well-being shaped the person you are today? Envision the legacy you wish to leave for future generations—spiritually, financially, academically, and in other aspects of life. Identify one action you can take today to contribute to building a better future for the next generation. It could be volunteering as a mentor, investing in educational resources, or simply sharing your knowledge and experiences with others. Next, commit to embodying the values of continuous learning and growth as you strive to make your next generation better than your own.

INTERACTIVE EXERCISE

Engage in storytelling sessions with your family, sharing stories of past generations and exploring the ways these narratives have influenced your family's journey. This can deepen your appreciation for your family's history.

TRANSFORMATION/ RESULTS

By acknowledging the sacrifices and contributions of those who came before you, you can work toward building a stronger foundation for future generations. You honor your ancestors by learning from their experiences and striving to make each generation better than the last. Your commitment to growth and progress is a testament to their legacy.

EMBRACING LIFELONG LEARNING

In life, each generation plays a vital role in shaping the trajectory of human progress. From the humble beginnings of our ancestors to the achievements of the present day, the journey toward a better future is paved with the collective efforts of those who came before us. As I reflect on the values instilled in me by my parents and the opportunities afforded to me through education in and outside of the classroom I am reminded of the importance of embracing lifelong learning as a catalyst for growth and advancement.

REFLECTIVE CHALLENGE

Consider the role of education in your own life journey. How has learning shaped your perspectives, opened doors to new opportunities, and empowered you to overcome obstacles? Reflect on moments of personal growth and transformation fueled by a commitment to continuous learning.

INTERACTIVE EXERCISE

Take inventory of your current learning journey. Identify areas where you feel inspired to expand your knowledge and skills, whether it's through formal education, self-study, or experiential learning. Set aside time each week to engage in activities that nourish your intellect and broaden your horizons. Reach out to mentors, join online communities, or enroll in courses that align with your interests and goals.

TRANSFORMATION/ RESULTS

As you embark on this journey of lifelong learning, remember the words of my father: "Every generation must be better." Embrace the opportunity to contribute to the ongoing legacy of progress and excellence, both for yourself and for generations to come.

SOARING BEYOND BOUNDARIES

LESSONS FROM KITE FLYING

Every year, I eagerly anticipate my Easter weekend —a time dedicated to flying kites with my family. This tradition, rooted in old-school craftsmanship by my uncle, fosters healthy competition among family members, challenging whose kite will stay up the longest and reach the highest altitudes. Yet, beyond the joy of the tradition lies a metaphor for life's journey.

The process begins with the careful creation of kites using copybook pages, each personalized with the initial of my first name. Just like in life, the foundation must be strong before setting out on a journey. The right wind conditions are essential for the kite to take flight—a reminder that timing and external factors play crucial roles in our endeavors.

Much like life's challenges, flying a kite isn't without obstacles. Entanglements can occur, symbolizing conflicts or unexpected hurdles. To mitigate entanglements, the family wisely chose a spacious, respectful environment where each member's boundaries were understood and respected. When entanglements did happen, the emphasis was on patience, addressing issues calmly, and sometimes, the necessity of cutting ties with others—an analogy for handling conflicts in life.

The tension that arises when kites are entangled serves as a metaphor for life's conflicts. Panicking and pulling in opposite directions may lead to breakage. Instead, a calm, parallel approach to the issue can help untangle the situation. The reminder to have a repair kit ready serves as a metaphor for relying on our spiritual foundation and the Creator for restoration and redemption.

Despite the risks, every year presents an opportunity to fly a kite. The challenge and joy of putting it up symbolizes the determination to face life's challenges. Some kites soar effortlessly, while others face obstacles. The crowded Savannah skies represent life's competitive landscapes, and not every beautifully designed kite gets its moment to shine.

The diversity of kites in the Savannah mirrors the variety of talents, skills, and ambitions in life. Not every kite, regardless of its design or size, gets the chance to soar. The unpredictable winds and turbulent conditions serve as a reminder that success is not solely determined by skills or qualifications. Sometimes, it's about being patient and seizing the right opportunity.

The metaphor extends to personal growth and career aspirations. Possessing certain qualifications doesn't guarantee success. Timing, like the right wind, is crucial. Sometimes, it's about being well-designed and patiently waiting for the perfect conditions to showcase your beauty and strength.

REFLECTIVE CHALLENGE

Consider the entanglements or conflicts you've faced in life. How did you handle them, and what lessons did you learn from those experiences? Reflect on the moments when you felt the wind was right for you to soar.

INTERACTIVE EXERCISE

Reflect on past conflicts or entanglements that you've experienced with family members, friends, or colleagues. Choose one scenario that stands out to you as a suitable practice scenario.

Assign roles to yourself and a trusted friend, family member, or coach who is willing to participate in the exercise with you. Briefly outline the scenario and establish clear guidelines for the role-play, emphasizing respect and open communication.

Act out the conflict scenario, taking turns portraying each role. Focus on maintaining a calm and composed demeanor, even when emotions run high.

Practice active listening, empathy, and assertiveness as you navigate the conflict. Seek to understand the other person's perspective and express your own thoughts and feelings with clarity and respect.

Experiment with different conflict resolution strategies, such as compromise, negotiation, or problem-solving, to find what works best for the situation.

After completing the role-play, take a moment to reflect on your experience. Consider what strategies were effective in resolving the conflict and what areas may need further improvement.

Write down your reflections in your notebook or journal, noting any insights or lessons learned from the exercise. If participating with a partner, provide constructive feedback to each other, focusing on strengths and areas for growth.

Carry forward the insights gained from the role-play into your real-life interactions. Practice applying the conflict resolution skills you've developed in future conflicts or challenging situations, aiming to maintain a calm and parallel approach grounded in patience, empathy, and assertiveness.

TRANSFORMATION/RESULT

Life's journey, much like flying a kite, involves preparation, navigating entanglements with patience, handling tensions with care, and waiting for the opportune moment to soar. Remember that with patience, a calm approach, and reliance on your spiritual foundation, you can navigate challenges and continue to soar.

REFLECTIONS ON A JOURNEY

Seventeen weeks, 17 posts later, I found myself reflecting on the inception of a journey that had been years in the making. What started as a mere thought, fueled by motivation, inspiration, and eventually an unequivocal instruction, had evolved into tangible action. As I look back, I marvel at the progression of this chapter in my life.

The journey took a significant turn when the right person arrived at the right time—a guide and mentor who played a crucial role in developing and ensuring that I took those initial steps. This chapter had grown, expanded, and matured through seventeen posts, a testament to the transformative power of taking action.

Reflecting on the experience, I realized the wealth of lessons and stories that every day brought. Life, with its twists and turns, offered something worth sharing—a nugget of wisdom, a moment of inspiration, or a revelation that contributed to the evolving narrative of this chapter.

Have you taken the time to reflect on your journey? Not

just the negatives, but also the positives that emerged from seemingly challenging situations. People encountered, experiences lived—these are the threads woven into the fabric of your unique chapter. Reflection invites gratitude for the growth achieved and the strength gained.

In the span of seventeen weeks, my position had shifted. What began as an idea now stands as a tangible reality, with seventeen posts marking the progress and at least one active follower joining the journey. The unfolding chapters promise more revelations, lessons, and experiences yet to be shared.

As the journey unfolds, I invite you to stay connected, to witness the next chapter and beyond. Together, we'll explore unknown territories, learn from the experiences, and unveil the untold stories that lie ahead.

REFLECTIVE CHALLENGE

Start each day by reflecting on three things you are grateful for. This will set a positive tone and cultivate an attitude of gratitude. This practice helps you focus on the positives in your life, even amidst challenges, fostering resilience and a sense of abundance.

INTERACTIVE EXERCISE

Collaborate with a trusted friend to develop a structured action plan for a 17-week journey. Take concrete steps toward your goals. Break down larger objectives into smaller, manageable tasks. Track your progress, celebrate milestones, and stay focused and motivated along the way.

TRANSFORMATION/ RESULTS

Through engaging in reflective challenges and interactive exercises, you will gain clarity of purpose and direction for your journey. You will begin to develop a deeper understanding of your motivations, values, and aspirations, enabling you to make informed decisions and take intentional action toward your goals.

About the Author

I am the first of seven children which has proven to be an advantage. Through the years I realised my true calling to be a transformational speaker. Little did I know that at a very tender age nurturing my younger siblings would have provided a platform for me to evolve into being a story teller, a teacher and a coach.

In this book, I am inspired to encourage readers to trust the next chapter of their lives as an essential element for their personal growth and fulfillment. From my perspective, trusting the next chapter of your life begins with embracing change, fostering resilience and adaptability, while enabling individuals to navigate life's uncertainties with grace and courage. Next, trusting in the journey empowers individuals to let go of past disappointments and setbacks, freeing them to embrace new opportunities and experiences. Then, by trusting in the next chapter, readers open themselves up to growth and self-discovery, unlocking their full potential and discovering new passions and talents. My fourth reason is that trusting in the next chapter cultivates a positive mindset, fostering optimism and hope for the future, even in the face of adversity. Further, it allows individuals to release control and surrender to the flow of life, leading to greater peace and inner contentment. In addition, trusting in the next chapter encourages individuals to take calculated risks and step out of their comfort zones, leading to personal and professional breakthroughs. My final reason is that it invites individuals to cultivate trust in themselves and their abilities, empowering them to create the life they envision and manifest their dreams into reality.

As you read, you are encouraged to participate in the significant reflective challenges and interactive exercises, and to trust the next chapter of your life with the intent of achieving transformational results.